THE UNIVERSE IN YOU

A Microscopic Journey

JASON CHIN

NEAL PORTER BOOKS

HOLIDAY HOUSE / NEW YORK

For Colin, Halle, and Andrew

Neal Porter Books

Text and illustrations copyright © 2022 by Jason Chin

All Rights Reserved

HOLIDAY HOUSE is registered in the U.S. Patent and Trademark Office.

Printed and bound in February 2023 at C&C Offset, Shenzhen, China.

The artwork for this book was created using watercolor, gouache, and digital techniques.

Book design by Jennifer Browne and Jason Chin

www.holidayhouse.com

First Edition

3   5   7   9   10   8   6   4   2

Library of Congress Cataloging-in-Publication Data

Names: Chin, Jason, 1978– author.

Title: The universe in you : a microscopic journey / by Jason Chin.

Description: First edition. | New York : Holiday House, [2022] | Includes
bibliographical references and index. | Audience: Ages 4 to 8

Audience: Grades K–1 | Summary: "A book exploring the world of the very
small, delving deep into the microscopic spaces just beneath our skin"—
Provided by publisher.

Identifiers: LCCN 2022015678 | ISBN 9780823450701 (hardcover)

Subjects: LCSH: Microstructure—Juvenile literature. | Cells—Juvenile
literature.

Classification: LCC QH273.2 .C45 2022 | DDC 571.6—dc23/eng/20220622

LC record available at https://lccn.loc.gov/2022015678

ISBN 978-0-8234-5070-1 (hardcover)

The Calliope Hummingbird is the smallest bird in the United States. At just 8 centimeters long from beak tip to tail, these tiny birds are small enough to fit . . .

. . . in your hand.

But they're not as small as the smallest butterfly. With a wingspan of 1.2 centimeters, this Western Pygmy Blue is smaller than a penny—but it's not as small as . . .

Centimeters
One inch is equal to 2.54 centimeters

Inch ▰▰▰▰▰▰
Centimeter ▰▰

. . . the smallest bee.

Perdita minima is less than 2 millimeters long. It's a quarter as long as a Western Pygmy Blue and about as long as a nickel is thick, but even this tiny bee isn't as small as . . .

Millimeters
A millimeter is 10 times smaller than a centimeter.

Centimeter ■■■■
Millimeter ▪

Microns
A micron is 1,000 times smaller than a millimeter.

. . . a vellus hair.

Everyone Is Hairy

An adult human has around 5 million hairs covering almost every part of their body. Much of the body is covered in tiny vellus hairs that are difficult to see.

The smallest hairs on your body are called vellus hairs. This one is just 30 microns across. That's thinner than the antennae of the smallest bee. But if you could look beneath the surface of your skin, you would see that even the smallest hair is not as small as . . .

. . . a skin cell.

Cells are the building blocks of your body. Different
parts of your body are made of different kinds of cells.
Your skin is made of millions of skin cells, each of which
is around 15 microns across. That's about half the width
of a vellus hair, but even skin cells are made of smaller parts.

A Universe of Cells

An adult human is estimated to have more than
30 trillion cells. That's more cells than there
are galaxies in the observable universe!

Bacteria

Bacteria are single-celled organisms and are generally considered to be the smallest living things on Earth. Most are not harmful, and it's normal for human skin to have thousands of bacterial cells per square centimeter. These bacteria are just 1 micron across.

A Layer of Protection

A rough layer of dead, flattened cells covers the surface of your skin. This layer protects the living cells beneath from harmful bacteria and viruses.

Cells are like tiny water balloons. They have an outer membrane that surrounds a jelly-like substance called cytoplasm. Suspended in the cytoplasm is the round cell nucleus, which is about 8 microns across. That's so small that more than 7,000 could fit on the period at the end of this sentence.

Melanin

Cell Nucleus

Cytoplasm
The semi-fluid material inside a cell

Cell Membrane
The boundary of the cell, enclosing the cytoplasm

Melanocyte
A melanocyte is a special type of skin cell that makes melanin and delivers it to other skin cells, where it forms a shield to protect the nucleus from the sun's harmful ultraviolet rays.

But the cell nucleus is gigantic compared to . . .

Melanin
Melanin shields the nucleus from the sun's harmful ultrraviolet rays.

Melanin and Skin Tone
The more melanin in a person's skin, the darker their skin will be. Spending time in the sun often causes the skin to make more melanin to protect its cells, resulting in a tan.

. . . everything else inside the cell.

Cells contain many different parts that all work together to keep the cell—and you—alive. They turn food into energy to power the cell, build new parts for your body, and recycle and remove waste. Cells are fantastically complicated living machines.

Newly made molecules are packaged and sent to their destination from the **Golgi Body**.

Organelles do different jobs in the life of the cell. The largest organelle is the cell nucleus, and the smallest are the lysosomes.

All of these parts are tiny. Mitochondria are about 1 micron across. Lysosomes are usually less than half a micron across. That's so small that more than 1,000,000 lysosomes could fit on the period at the end of this sentence. But even they are big compared to . . .

Melanin

Lysosomes clean up the cell by breaking down old cell parts.

Many new molecules are constructed in the **Endoplasmic Reticulum.**

The **Cell Nucleus is** home to the cell's DNA and is covered with nuclear pores.

The **Cytoskeleton** is a network of thin filaments that gives the cell structure, like beams in a building. Some filaments double as pathways for cellular machines that transport material around the cell.

Mitochondria turn food and oxygen into energy for the cell.

. . . nuclear pores.

Nuclear pores are found on the surface of the cell nucleus. They are gateways that ensure only the right materials can pass in and out. They are less than 150 nanometers across, which is so small that more than 2,000 of them can fit on the cell nucleus. But even nuclear pores are made of smaller parts called . . .

Nuclear Pore

New Molecule

Messenger RNA

Ribosomes
Ribosomes are biological machines that assemble many new molecules inside your cells. To build a new molecule, they follow instructions in messenger RNA.

Nanometers
A nanometer is 1,000 times smaller than a micron.

A Supercharged Ball Pit
The cytoplasm is like a supercharged ball pit. It's filled with millions of molecules moving at incredible speeds—many rotate a million times per second!

Messenger RNA

Nuclear Membrane
Millions of molecules join together to form the membrane.

Nuclear Pore

. . . molecules.

Molecules are the building blocks of every part of the cell. It takes hundreds of molecules to make a nuclear pore, millions to make the nuclear membrane, and each of your cells contains billions of water molecules. But the longest molecules in your body are packed inside the cell nucleus. They're called . . .

. . . DNA.

DNA is a long twisting molecule that contains your genetic code—the information your cells need to build and maintain your body. If all of the DNA molecules in just one of your cells were stretched out, they would be about two meters long. But DNA is just two nanometers wide—about 15,000 times thinner than a vellus hair. And like all molecules they are made up of even smaller parts called . . .

Your Genes

Your DNA contains many sections of code called genes. Genes are instructions for building molecules that your body needs to live and grow.

Reading the Code

Genes are recipes for molecules. This biological machine is reading a gene and making a copy of the recipe. The copy, called messenger RNA, will be used to make new molecules.

. . . atoms.

Atoms are the building blocks of molecules. Different types of atoms are called elements, and they are all less than one nanometer across. The smallest atoms in your body are hydrogen atoms at just one-tenth of a nanometer across. That's 20 times thinner than a strand of DNA, but even atoms are made of smaller parts.

Hydrogen Atom

Oxygen Atom

Phosphorus Atom

Carbon Atom

Every atom is made of an atomic nucleus surrounded by an electron cloud. The electron cloud is where particles called electrons are found. The nucleus is at the center of the cloud, but it's far too small to see at this scale. The nucleus in a hydrogen atom is about 60,000 times smaller than the atom itself. It is made of a single particle called . . .

Atomic Nucleus
The nucleus is in the center of the atom, but it's too small to see in this picture.

Electron Cloud
Electron clouds are made of electrons. Electrons are even smaller than protons and are very strange. They behave as if they are in many places at once, so even a single electron can form an entire electron cloud!

. . . a proton.

This is a proton enlarged more than 1 trillion times its actual size. If the proton were this big, the atom would be the size of a football field! Protons are about 0.0000017 nanometers across, making them among the smallest objects that scientists have ever measured, but even protons aren't as small as . . .

Proton
If the proton were this big,
the atom would be more
than 100 meters across.

Protons and Neutrons
Hydrogen atoms have one proton in their nucleus,
but all other elements have more than one.
Other elements also have neutrons, which
are particles similar to protons.

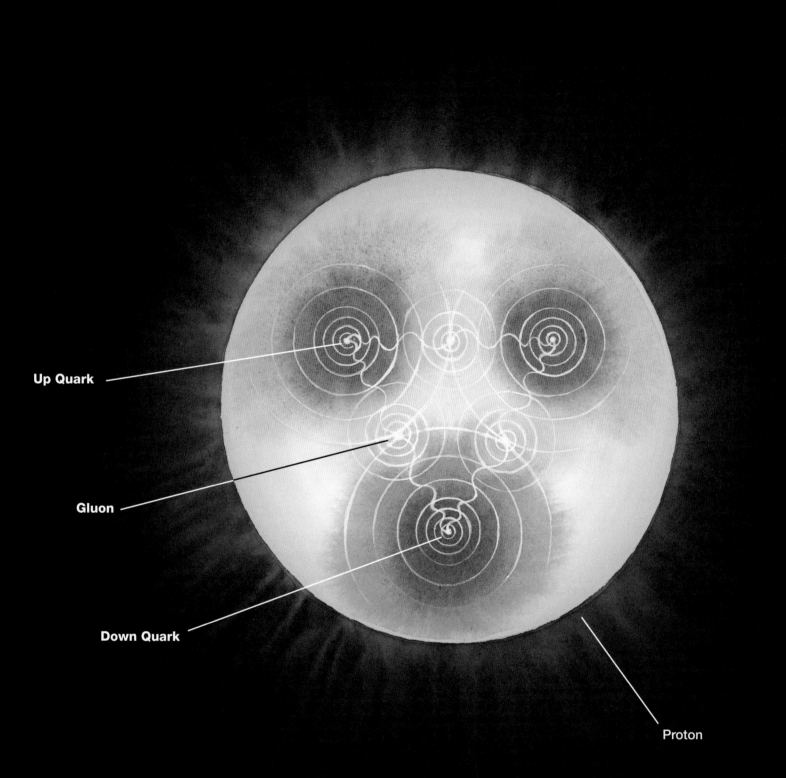

Up Quark

Gluon

Down Quark

Proton

Atoms Are Made of Elementary Particles
Protons are made of three quarks (two up and
one down) that are bound together by gluons.
Electrons in the electron cloud are also
elementary particles.

. . . elementary particles.

Protons are made of elementary particles called quarks and gluons. These particles are so small that no one has ever been able to measure their size, and they've never been divided into smaller parts. Elementary particles are the smallest things known to science and are the basic building blocks of . . .

Elementary Particles Are Weird

Elementary particles aren't like any objects we are familiar with. They can tunnel through barriers, blink in and out of existence, and behave as if they are in many places at once. They are so small, they may not have any size at all! Nobody has a complete understanding of these strange particles, which is exactly why scientists study them.

. . . the universe.

Elementary particles are the building blocks of all physical matter. They make every atom, and atoms make every molecule in every galaxy, star, and planet.

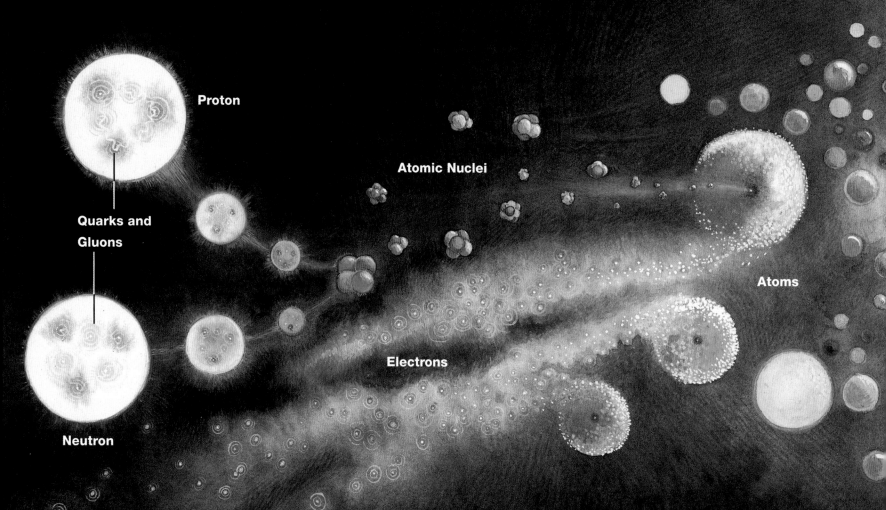

Proton

Quarks and Gluons

Neutron

Atomic Nuclei

Electrons

Atoms

Elementary Particles Make Atoms
Quarks and gluons make up the protons and neutrons in the atomic nucleus. Electrons surround the nucleus in the electron cloud. Several other particles (not pictured) carry the forces that hold the atom together.

The Elements
There are 118 different types of atoms, or elements. Different elements have different numbers of protons in their nuclei.

Atoms and molecules combine to make Earth and everything on it, from the air you breathe to the water you drink, from the ground beneath your feet . . .

Molecules

When atoms bind together, they make molecules. When atoms of two different elements bind together, the molecule is called a compound.

. . . to life itself.

Molecules combine to make cells,
which are the building blocks
of living organisms.

Molecules Make Cells
It takes millions of molecules to construct
a cell. Water molecules are the most
common and make up around
70 percent of a human cell.

All living things, from the tallest
trees and longest whales . . .

Cells and Life
It's commonly said that all living things are
made of cells, but many scientists argue that
viruses are also alive even though they
aren't made of cells.

. . . to the smallest birds, butterflies,
and bees, are made of cells—
just like you.

You are made of the same stuff as everything else in the universe. Your body is made of the same particles that make stars. It contains the same elements that make the air and the ocean. The same molecules that are found in your cells are found in butterflies and hummingbirds.

But you are none of these things.

The Elements in You

The four most common elements in your body are hydrogen, nitrogen, oxygen, and carbon. The sun is made mostly of hydrogen. The air is made mostly of nitrogen and oxygen. The element carbon is the basis of the molecules found in every cell on Earth.

Your particles, atoms, and molecules are arranged into cells that are arranged into tissues and organs that form the body of a unique human being . . .

a singular person, who can think
and feel and discover . . .

. . . the universe within.

THE BUILDING BLOCKS OF MATTER

Matter is anything that takes up space and has mass. Everything around you—this book, your body, and even the air you breathe—is made of matter. Elementary particles are the building blocks of matter. They make up atoms, which make up molecules, which combine to make objects large enough for us to see.

ATOMS

Every atom has an atomic nucleus surrounded by an electron cloud. The nucleus is made of protons and neutrons. The electron cloud is made of one or more electrons, which are elementary particles and are very small. In fact, most of the cloud, and therefore most of the atom, is empty space! But electrons behave as if they are in many places at once, so even a single electron can make an entire electron cloud. This is an example of the strange behavior of elementary particles.

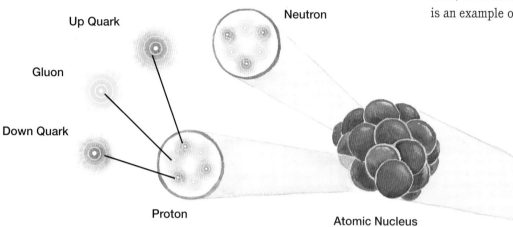

Up Quark

Neutron

Gluon

Down Quark

Proton

Atomic Nucleus

Electrons

Oxygen Atom

ELEMENTARY PARTICLES

There are 17 known elementary particles. They are the smallest things known to science and the fundamental building blocks of matter. In addition to making up atoms, they give rise to the forces that hold atoms together, and account for phenomena like light, electricity, and magnetism. These particles don't behave like anything we are familiar with. They are very difficult to understand and there is still a lot to learn about them.

THE ATOMIC NUCLEUS

Protons and neutrons make up the nuclei of atoms, and they are very small. If a proton were the size of a blueberry, the atom would be taller than the Empire State Building! Despite being very small, the nucleus accounts for 99.9 percent of the atom's mass. Different elements have different numbers of protons in their nuclei. A hydrogen atom contains one proton, an oxygen atom contains eight protons, and gold contains 79 protons.

The 17 Known Elementary Particles

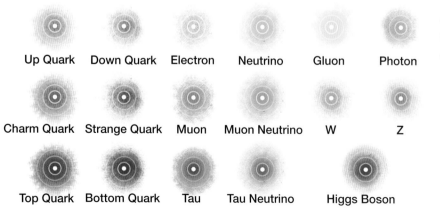

Up Quark	Down Quark	Electron	Neutrino	Gluon	Photon
Charm Quark	Strange Quark	Muon	Muon Neutrino	W	Z
Top Quark	Bottom Quark	Tau	Tau Neutrino	Higgs Boson	

Hydrogen

Oxygen

Gold

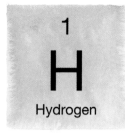

1 H																	2 He
3 Li	4 Be											5 B	6 C	7 N	8 O	9 F	10 Ne
11 Na	12 Mg											13 Al	14 Si	15 P	16 S	17 Cl	18 Ar
19 K	20 Ca	21 Sc	22 Ti	23 V	24 Cr	25 Mn	26 Fe	27 Co	28 Ni	29 Cu	30 Zn	31 Ga	32 Ge	33 As	34 Se	35 Br	36 Kr
37 Rb	38 Sr	39 Y	40 Zr	41 Nb	42 Mo	43 Tc	44 Ru	45 Rh	46 Pd	47 Ag	48 Cd	49 In	50 Sn	51 Sb	52 Te	53 I	54 Xe
55 Cs	56 Ba	57-71 *	72 Hf	73 Ta	74 W	75 Re	76 Os	77 Ir	78 Pt	79 Au	80 Hg	81 Tl	82 Pb	83 Bi	84 Po	85 At	86 Rn
87 Fr	88 Ra	89-103 **	104 Rf	105 Db	106 Sg	107 Bh	108 Hs	109 Mt	110 Ds	111 Rg	112 Cn	113 Nh	114 Fl	115 Mc	116 Lv	117 Ts	118 Og

*	57 La	58 Ce	59 Pr	60 Nd	61 Pm	62 Sm	63 Eu	64 Gd	65 Tb	66 Dy	67 Ho	68 Er	69 Tm	70 Yb	71 Lu
**	89 Ac	90 Th	91 Pa	92 U	93 Np	94 Pu	95 Am	96 Cm	97 Bk	98 Cf	99 Es	100 Fm	101 Md	102 No	103 Lr

PERIODIC TABLE OF THE ELEMENTS

The periodic table lists every element according to the number of protons in its nucleus. The first 92 occur naturally. The remaining elements were either made in a lab or are exceedingly rare in nature.

THE ELEMENTS

There are 118 known elements. Each has a different number of protons in its nucleus, and each has different properties. Hydrogen is a transparent gas, gold is a lustrous metal, and so on. An atom is the smallest unit of any element—a ring made of billions of gold atoms is gold, but so is a single gold atom. The Periodic Table of the Elements is a chart of every known atom.

BORN IN STARS

In the beginning of the universe only a few elements existed: hydrogen and a small amount of helium and lithium. Every other element was made later, inside of stars. The interior of stars is so hot that atomic nuclei are split apart and then fused into new elements. This means that, aside from those three elements, the atoms in your body were all born inside of stars!

MOLECULES

Molecules are built out of atoms, and there are seemingly limitless ways to combine atoms into molecules. A molecule made of different elements is called a compound, and compounds can be very different from the elements that make them. For example, hydrogen and oxygen are both gases, but when put together they make water. Small molecules like water are made of just a few atoms, while large molecules (called macromolecules) can have millions of atoms!

Water molecules are made of one oxygen atom and two hydrogen atoms. Water molecules are so small that it takes about 7,900,000,000,000,000,000,000,000 molecules to fill a single cup of water!

Water
Molecule

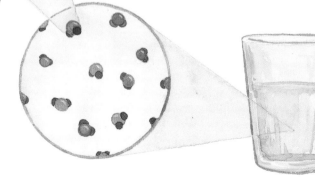

Carbon Dioxide

Phospholipid

Ozone

Vitamin C

THE BUILDING BLOCKS OF LIFE

Cells are the building blocks of living organisms. Your body has around 200 different kinds of cells, which form different tissues like muscle, fat, and bone. Organs, such as your heart, are made of different tissues. Multiple organs make up organ systems, such as the nervous system. All the systems together form your body.

THE CELL

There are many different types of cells in your body, and most have the same basic structure. An outer cell membrane surrounds the cytoplasm and the cell nucleus. Organelles in the cell carry out different life processes, such as converting food to energy, making new molecules, and removing waste.

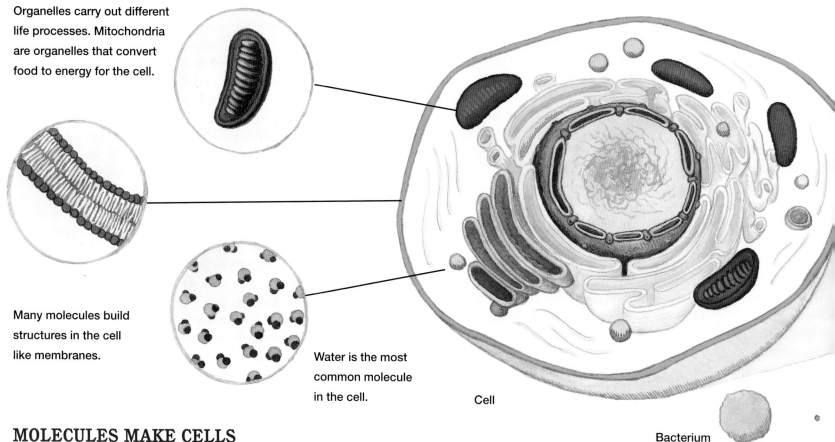

Organelles carry out different life processes. Mitochondria are organelles that convert food to energy for the cell.

Many molecules build structures in the cell like membranes.

Water is the most common molecule in the cell.

Cell

Bacterium

Virus

MOLECULES MAKE CELLS

Cells are made of many different molecules. The most common are water molecules, which make up around 70 percent of the cell. The remainder of the cell is made mostly of organic molecules that are only found in living things. Different molecules have different roles. Some make cell structures, such as membranes, while others perform tasks. Kinesin is a molecular machine that transports material around the cell by "walking" along the cytoskeleton. Ribosomes are machines made of many molecules, and they assemble new molecules.

A kinesin molecule "walks" along the cytoskeleton

THE SMALLEST LIFE

Single-celled bacteria and a similar group called archaea are the world's smallest cells, and they live everywhere: high in the atmosphere, deep underground, and all over our bodies. There are so many bacteria and archaea, that, put together, they'd weigh more than every animal on Earth! Viruses are roughly ten times smaller than bacteria, and there are even more of them on Earth: an estimated 10 million billion quadrillion (that's a 10 with 30 zeros after it)! Viruses don't eat or reproduce on their own. Instead, they inject their genetic material into cells and trick the cells into making new viruses. The vast majority of bacteria and viruses aren't harmful to humans, but if they do infect us, our immune systems have many tools for fighting them off.

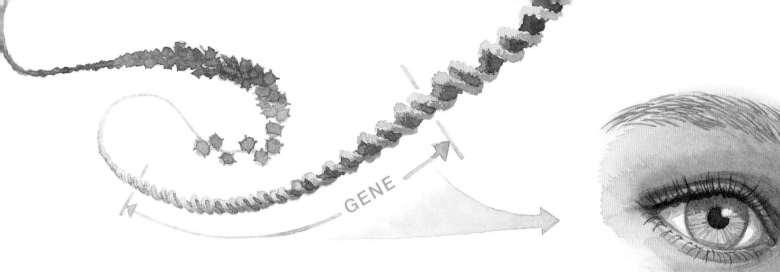

DNA AND GENES

DNA molecules hold all of the information necessary for building and maintaining your body. Every strand of DNA has sections called genes. Each gene is like a recipe. It's a set of instructions for making a specific molecule for your body. Each molecule has a specific role to play in how your body functions. All together, you have 20,000 to 25,000 genes!

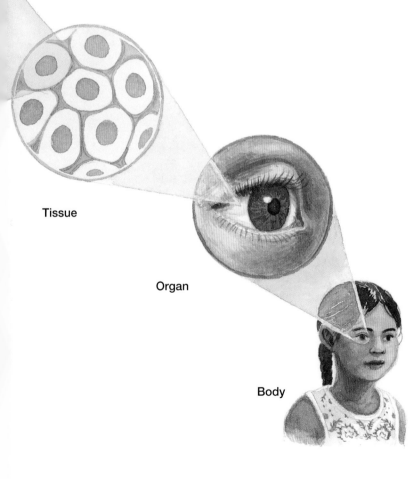

Tissue

Organ

Body

GENES AND PHYSICAL TRAITS

All of the information contained in your DNA is called your genome. All humans have nearly identical genomes. In fact, your genome is 99.9 percent the same as that of every other human on Earth. The small fraction that is different contributes to the variation in physical traits between different people. For example, we all have genes that code for molecules to help make melanin. Variations in these genes cause different people to produce different amounts of melanin, giving them different skin, hair, and eye color.

Genes play a large role in our physical traits, but they aren't the only factors at work. Lifestyle and environmental factors also influence how your body develops. Your DNA may be a recipe book for your body, but it's just part of what makes you you.

WHAT IS LIFE?

Living things, regardless of size, perform certain functions. These include consuming energy; building, organizing, and maintaining their bodies; reproduction; and undergoing evolution over time. Organisms made of cells are the only things on Earth that do all of these things, so it's often said that all life is made of cells. But many scientists consider viruses to be alive, even though they do not do all of these things. Viruses are organized and they evolve, but they don't eat and can't reproduce on their own. Whether or not viruses are alive depends on how you define "life," and there is no definition that every scientist agrees with.

A NOTE FROM THE AUTHOR

When I think about the scale of our universe and its many billions of stars and galaxies, I often feel overwhelmed, but when I think about smaller scales, the experience is even more mind-boggling. There are more cells in your body than there are galaxies in the observable universe. At the smallest scale, scientists have found something even more amazing: all matter is constructed of the same handful of parts. The same particles that make stars also make this book, and make your hands and eyes and brain. In this sense, the universe is in you, just as you are in it. You are a bunch of particles and atoms just like this book, but you are so much more than that. You have the ability to understand who and what you are, and to dream, imagine, and learn. You are one of a kind, a piece of the universe unlike any other.

A NOTE ON THE ILLUSTRATIONS

I have tried to make my illustrations true to reality, but there are three important ways in which my images do not look like the real thing. First, real cells are crowded. In my pictures I left out many of the molecules and other structures so you can see the parts I wrote about. Second, much of the world at microscopic scales is colorless, but I added color to my pictures to make different structures easier to see. Finally, the images of elementary particles are completely invented. This is because elementary particles are impossible for human brains to visualize, so *any* picture of them is not accurate. My images are symbols of particles, but they do not look like the real thing.

ACKNOWLEDGMENTS

I would like to thank the following experts for their help with the research and fact-checking of this book. I could not have completed it without them:

Billy Braasch, PhD, Department of Physics, Dartmouth College
Andrea Lee, PhD, Department of Microbiology and Molecular Genetics and the Department of Chemistry, University of Vermont
Juan Vanegas, PhD, Department of Physics, University of Vermont
Michele von Turkovich, BA, laboratory/research technician senior, University of Vermont College of Medicine, Microscopy Imaging Center
David Warshaw, PhD, Chair of the Department of Molecular Physiology and Biophysics, University of Vermont
Christine Weinberger, MD, Associate Professor of Dermatology, University of Vermont

Special thanks to Kelly Brush Davisson, President of the Kelly Brush Foundation. Please visit kellybrushfoundation.org to learn how the Kelly Brush Foundation helps individuals with spinal cord injuries pursue active lifestyles.

SELECTED SOURCES

BOOKS

Alberts, Bruce, Dennis Bray, Julian Lewis, Martin Raff, Keith Roberts, and James D. Watson. *Molecular Biology of the Cell*. 3rd ed. New York: Garland Science, 1994.

CERN, "The Standard Model: The Standard Model explains how the basic building blocks of matter interact, governed by four fundamental forces." https://home.cern/science/physics/standard-model. Accessed June 28, 2021.

Fayer, Michael D. *Absolutely Small: How Quantum Theory Explains Our Everyday World*. New York: AMACOM, 2010.

Goodsell, David S. *The Machinery of Life*. 2nd Ed. New York: Springer, 2009.

Gray, Theodore. *The Elements: A Visual Exploration of Every Known Atom in the Universe*. New York: Black Dog & Leventhal, 2009.

———. *Molecules: The Elements and the Architecture of Everything*. New York: Black Dog & Leventhal, 2014.

Marieb, Elaine N. *Human Anatomy and Physiology*. 5th ed. New York: Benjamin Cummings, 2001.

Milo, Ron, Paul Jorgensen, Uri Moran, Griffin Weber, and Michael Springer. "BioNumbers—the database of key numbers in molecular and cell biology." Nucleic Acids Research 38, Database issue (2010): D750-3. doi:10.1093/nar/gkp889.

Ryan, Morgan, Gaël McGill, and Edward O. Wilson. *E.O. Wilson's Life on Earth*. E.O. Wilson Biodiversity Foundation, 2014. Apple iBook.

National Human Genome Research Institute. "Introduction to Genomics: What's a Genome?" https://www.genome.gov/About-Genomics/Introduction-to-Genomics. Accessed October 25, 2021.